Some
frames

Some
frames

jack
hannan

poems

Cormorant Books

The publisher gratefully acknowledges the support of the Canada Council for the Arts and the
Ontario Arts Council for its publishing program. We acknowledge the financial support of
the Government of Canada through the Canada Book Fund (CBF) for our publishing activities,
and the Government of Ontario through the Ontario Media Development Corporation, an agency of
the Ontario Ministry of Culture, and the Ontario Book Publishing Tax Credit Program.

LIBRARY AND ARCHIVES CANADA CATALOGUING IN PUBLICATION

Hannan, Jack
Some frames : poems / Jack Hannan.

ISBN 978-1-77086-005-6

1. Title.

PS8565.A585S66 2011   C811'.54   C2011-900012-1

The cover illustration is a painting (undated) by Johanna Dowling Griffin,
courtesy of Jack Hannan, her grandson.

Cover design: Angel Guerra/Archetype
Interior text design: Tannice Goddard, Soul Oasis Networking
Printer: Sunville Printco Inc.

Printed and bound in Canada.

CORMORANT BOOKS INC.
215 SPADINA AVENUE, STUDIO 230, TORONTO, ONTARIO, CANADA M5T 2C7
www.cormorantbooks.com

Contents

Note

So it turns out that I am not such a prolific writer. There are some people who write a dozen books and feel that they can't get anything done. I try to cheer them on. I have always liked chapbooks, small books of four or five or even a dozen poems. I like to read them, to hold them in my hands, I like having them around the house. And I was always very happy to see my work published that way, in such little books. There's a pleasure even in three copies of a piece of paper folded in half. It's a good tradition to be a part of. I hold them out to my friends. There's a convenient symmetry in this, I know, an interesting logic in the man who writes so little preferring little books. Am I the chicken or the egg?

In 1984, I stopped writing for about twenty years, and then slowly started again.

There were four small books, and they are reprinted here pretty much as they originally appeared, each chapbook under its own title. There is a section called "Some frames," collecting new and some older poems that never appeared in chapbooks, though some were published in magazines. Among the new poems is a sequence called Dwayne's poems. Dwayne Murphy is a fictional character, a young poet in a novel I have written, and these are some of his poems.

This book is dedicated to Deborah, Jesse, and Molly.
I hold it out in my hands.

Jack Hannan
MONTREAL, JUNE 2010

I

Some frames

All those moons

Who put all those moons up there
and then made your foot twitch like that
when you're bored, sometimes
days are as populous as cities, or towns, anyway,
if not exactly exuberant with parades, at least there
beside you on the street, whole tolerant lifetimes
walking hand in hand, magnified many times
in mirrors, who put all those stars in the sky
and what makes your eyes look like that
when you're surprised, imagine a man
on a low dark platform, a makeshift stage,
it looks like night,
he exaggerates everything he does,
he does, he's digging his hands
deep into a large pail and then heaving
stars into the air like water
all the stars his arms can hold
whole armloads of shining stars and crescent moons
glistening in the night, he throws them out over the crowd
like a fisherman throws his net out over the sea
the children are in awe, their mouths agape
whose idea was it that their laughter should sound like that
when all the green vegetables rise up through the floor to sing "eat me"
imagine a man and a woman in a factory
dancing between those lime green machines that are used to make stars
for people alone with their thoughts
on the
sidewalk
there is a densely populated man
on a small low stage in a children's school, it looks like night,
on the stage there is a lamp
with two garbage cans, he walks
between the kids sitting on the floor to the stage

he reaches into one pail and pulls out a bird and a comet
he throws them high into the air
he finds a feather boa, a planet on a stick
a long green plant, how did that even fit,
he puts on a hat
he finds a blue tricycle, a child wonders *will*
there be animals?
he throws a full moon, he throws a milky string of stars
a little boy stands up alone and calls out
"That's not the real moon,"
and silence, crestfallen,
all the other children around him nod their heads
it's true they decide
that's not the real moon

Some frames

There are five frames, negatives, with a bird
in the fourth frame from the left, the way the eye reads,
water, or it might be clouds
under the wings spread wide, rising from the tips
the sun is in the fifth frame, or anyway something
round, a planet
the moon, a plate, there is
this dark strip of negatives that turns brown or slightly orange in the light
on a table, stuck between the pages of a magazine

The sun is in the fifth frame, a last fragment
statement, a summing up
a bird is in the fourth, the bird
seems to be slowly climbing, or slightly inclining
nothing is in the first frame
and the others have what looks like clouds,
cotton or tumbleweeds or dust or water
rolling partway up each frame, you don't even know
who these belong to, and it's not so obvious
why someone is keeping them or someone left them

There was one cookie with
two fortunes, already fortunate, no? However
they both say the same thing, "you have
a quiet and unobtrusive nature"
everyone had a good laugh at that, you are
almost not there at all, and twice! we wondered
if it was a matter of language, this may be
an important and traditional compliment in some cultures
but less in our own, though maybe still
appreciated, just a little vacant, victims, people about to go postal

Curling slivers of colored plastic, turning the way worms
turn the earth inside our wordy hearts, friends
will begin again, out into the narrative light of morning, slivers,
the skin of an orange in twisty
arcane pieces, looking for ways to start again
there is a strip of five negatives
in a row, they are all similar
and they do not seem to lead from one to another
exactly, simple changes in each
apparently through someone's pleasant day

A bird indicates the sun
these windows bring the ocean's tumbling waves
the way that you bring me
dusty, hands
smelling of orange, quiet and
do you still recognize me when I am so unobtrusive?
The way that I have brought you here
to the ocean, a small and sandy line, when you wake the sun
will have already warmed this red and fortunate world
and I am already and still waiting

For you. Sometimes it seems that all that was all
just this, a winding line through years can be just
one long eventful day's passing, and jam enough
to spread on toast, unless
we step to the side, and a jumble of flow,
rise and fall, high and low, ebb and
la dee dah, time
is letting you sleep longer than I like, obviously,
it's clear that together
we are an engine of variable speeds

Roiling clouds slowly gave way and the sky cleared
we all thought the abandoned rooms had been emptied
quietly, a long time ago,
the doors and windows were painted
shut, *we are cleaning nothing*
on a regular basis, we are dusting the air,
people played football on the lawn, they drank
a lot of alcohol and they talked about food
we grew specific, descriptive, though
unimportant, no one cared really

Cities engulfed in waves, mouths full of marbles, is this
what you call getting lost, have you a name for this
that you could tell us,
why are you returning now, and I only vaguely wonder
what are you leaving somewhere else this time, what coast
are you flying in from, as welcome
as you are, and you are, these are just questions, I know
the island changes shape and color in your presence
we all come alive in you, though not
all at once, one after another as you turn to us, like frames

You are a lamp in the meaningless way, you are a light, a glow
in the darkness that knows us so well
why would a person want to entertain such loss
and is that then what makes a person look toward emptiness
silence, abstinence, stone, rock, concrete
none of these are nothing and this is your music
of acquired taste, we can hear it through the trees
from far away as we approach
very curious, but outside still and always
even when we arrive we remain outsiders in welcome

We are as shiny as mirrors in your light
even when we arrive there's this uneasy question of
who is actually present
one passes a doubtful hand
in strange aggressive motions inches over another's body
I can't feel you here at all
and one looks into the other's eyes and yes it's true
then *slowly, there is this music that seems to know me*
I have this sense of being stared at, you know
this feeling like I am not alone

As ever we continue to narrate in our own manner
the quiet and unobtrusive days within us
will you inhabit me as that bird
lives in those frames,
others will hardly notice, all of us in our uniform ways,
one rose and thought of the other's presence
did the other dream this happened, or does the whole
turn in some sleepy, waking gesture
the catalpas unfurl their finger-like pods in waiting
their exuberant clusters of churchy white flowers

By the side of the woods, stopping
like some little Robert Frost with a big idea
about Emily Dickinson, catalpa speciosa, the bird,
a hawk, a falcon glides
slowly, away or closer, toward the left,
the sun is behind you, a man looking up
has this feeling that things are all right
still and again, and it is surprising for him to think of this, the sun
fills the fifth frame in his hands
the earth italicizes itself and everything rises in greeting

The opening in a fence is your most attractive
quality, the fingers of mop-head catalpas at the side
of an old building, vines, ivy,
we are in this familiar and yet unusual arcade and in your garden at once
and these things also quickly become part of you now
for me, or become my way of explaining,
though that's not exactly the word, imagining, calling
to all of this for both you and me
both the garden and the arcade have been engulfed
waves roll halfway up the frames

We hold these mirrors to the light of a smooth and
lustrous moment, a finite suggestion, a few
words, some grow so quiet in their dedication
measuring boulders, mountains before them, we forget
they were ever here, they disappear, how will I fit, where
will I put my fingers, they are gone, some
flicker into the tangible distance, I have turned my back
for a very long time and I believed
I had been forgotten, but oh no
you are so rampant it's ridiculous

We are these silvery mirrors angled to look
around corners and down long hallways
toward a vast and entangled surface
and we are all eventually some red-cheeked man
leaning on his drum in the morning, puffy and waiting
for a friend to wake, and when you do wake I ask
let me be glass, this day let yourself
shine through me like the spark in an eye, let the others
walk through me the way we walk through waves of shimmering light
fine white sand and lime translucent as glass

Who asks for all this, a couple of people
walking away from the house in the early morning
a conversation among rhythms, the other
reaches across unlikely distances, maybe it is possible
that I really can hear you breathing
I can somehow already make out your silhouette
there in those waves of water and heat rising
I am finding you but I'm not the only one
we are all coming alive in these stories of your presence
and I feel that you too have been waiting

Here you can see the frames of water and heat
and now will there be no turning away
the clear air is yet visible in the waves of light
and tangible on the soft surface of your skin
Good morning Van Winkle and welcome
how are you feeling today, waking in these old buildings, these
mornings of a thin silver chain at your neck, half-buildings,
parts of brick walls, standing side-by-side in catalpa trees, a pony
standing near a fence in the ornamental grass,
you know you could have woken me sooner

Huddles of people slumping like string puppets
around corners, vacant reflections
in mirrors and then slowly at first
but later more quickly this is all left behind, all these
warehouses with their clanging chains and people shouting, nervous
energy pulling us upright, zam, wooden limbs a-clonking
and we start having these dreams of flying, soaring
across oceans, waves as high as homes
thick cities bright in the night with rivers and mountains
in their distances dense with snow

A woman walks from the house in the morning
toward the water, she gestures, she sits on a rock
beside a man, while they talk about cadence he is watching
her hands, her arms, the way she stretches her legs, he listens
to her breathing, she gives him
pieces of orange, they have reached
across improbable distances, and now
he follows her gaze out toward the trees, an arcade of languages
is hovering expansive around them, buzzing, waves
crash on the stones almost at their feet

People walking on a path near the trees, or maybe through curtains
of smooth light hanging in the dusty air
in a building with a large empty room, do we
walk through these projections in the dark air
or do you go around them,
do you want the light
to shine on your own skin, is that
how it's supposed to go or not
we drop our bodies slowly
into the water, we walk through the shining light

We are these quiet greetings, unobtrusive weight, a low white fence,
shadows, crashing waves
hanging in the air touching their skin
curtains of smooth light hanging in the air
visible in a building with an old dusty room
where I know you best, do we
walk through these objects or do you go around them
do you want the light to shine on your own skin, is that
how it's supposed to go
we move our bodies slowly into the light, we slip down into the water

A couple of people by a low fence, in a long dark room
with pools of light, a line of sand
wings are spread across your shoulders, waves
or tumbleweed curl over my arms, two people
walk up onto a roof, by a fence near the catalpa trees, one turned
in all directions, the other grew into a spiral
I think you are a vibrant truth, though I know, right,
who talks like that? You are pouring water into the glass
that will never be full, or drinking from the glass
that will never empty, I think you are a vibrant spiral

Untitled art advertisement #39

Sometimes I think of Mark Rothko with that grin
walking along 8th Avenue with his friend Barnett Newman
how many million people, where does this all end,
New York can be the craziest city in the world and yet Rothko
    paints these colour fields
like there's no one around at all, no joke
all is silent, enormous and beautiful flat panels, people
can sometimes think it's boring but they're wrong, to be alone
with one for an hour is very lucky, just sit and be quiet,
don't call it anything, they called it Abstract Expressionism, Rothko said
it's a lot like the backgrounds in a Rembrandt painting
but it's not really a lot like that, maybe a little,
New York surrounds him with energy, noise and things and people
    and wonder
he can hear the clatter of the city's own brain, the whole country
crashes around, but not here,
in 1971 Rothko was asked to work on a little building,
an art sanctuary, it is now called The Rothko Chapel
it's at the corner of Yupon and Sul Ross Streets, in Houston, Texas,
the chapel is built around 14 of Rothko's most ominous paintings
you can feel so alone and cold there at first and then later again not, and
    right outside
there's a sculpture by Barnett Newman, called The Broken Obelisk,
anyway, this is another nice place to be alone
if ever you feel you'd like to be alone in Houston, Texas

A person like Clifford George

I would like to speak to Clifford George
dumping trunk-loads of his books into the St. Lawrence River, all of his books,
Why? Did he feel relief? Did he sigh? It's easy to imagine
he was angry, but at what?
He was a fist, two fists at the end of his reach, did he later become
a more active participant in the blossoming flower of existence?
What was inactive before?
You're an inquisitive guy, huh,
you like to ask questions?
Today I imagine that I could talk to Clifford George
I am the one beside him helping unload the car
but I stop to read the titles, *can I have this?*
frivolous even to myself, there's a little pile of books on the rocks
and I know he wants to scoop them up with everything else,
feel the tension in his body, this was in 1934
he was wearing a coat and a wide-brimmed hat
he wore a tie that I'd like to have now,
I wait for him by the water while he goes to get another load, and I wonder
what is this that we're doing? is this a fury of denial
or is this a wild affirmation?
How do we come to believe we are so wrong, or
we have been so wrong but do we think that later today
we will be all right?
This is a big question and I only have a few minutes,
still, it is something I know a little about,
I could join your weekly flailing meetings if you'd like,
Clifford leaves in the car and he does not come back, I sit
by the water alone with a lot of books, night is here,
I have made a mistake and been left behind, if I hadn't
taken so many books he would have at least driven me back into town,

I think of hiding the books in the bushes, but
from whom? I throw the books out into the water and
walk all the way home, it takes a long time, years later
there's a cement dock, a few boats,
I stand there again at the edge of the water, someone asks what I want

A poem in the kitchen

Today I bring home chocolate bees
penne, a baguette, garlic and milk,
today I heard a man say something to a woman while passing
she answered him quietly, and then he said very clearly
"Oh, you look Cree,"
and I wonder do Crees look different from Mohawks, or Micmaqs?
I don't even know anyone I can ask about that
is it like Americans and Canadians?
Today I saw a homeless bohemian sleeping in the hallway of the metro
he had a blanket and there was a Toblerone chocolate bar
on the floor near his hand,
today I saw a girl who looked just like you twenty-six years ago
I watched her for as long as I could, from an acceptable distance,
she was with a boy who did not look anything like me at all
I guess she's not there yet, eh?
I work for the government but I have to say
subways and buses are the strangest thing I do all day
people asleep in a crowd, bodies only inches away from their heads, the air
is full of breathing, people reading
over your shoulder, the noise
of a boy bouncing a basketball on the subway platform
while the rest of us wait and listen, it's loud!
Someone's little tiny earphones going
chuss chuss chuss chuss chuss
today there were two homeless bohemians sleeping in the hallway of the metro
and this morning there was a muffin in a little plastic baggy
in the hat near one of their hands,
a man says "well, if it's interesting, I'll smoke it" and
his companion laughs "Oh, I can't believe that," she says
there is a little girl holding the man's hand

two young people are talking about their school work, one finally
looks into space and says
"Fucking Milton,"
there's always some angle
that we shouldn't look at another person's body from,
today I heard our own daughter say "actually
it's all dangerous
but you know,"
today the young man who sleeps on the floor
in the corridor of the subway had a banana and an apple near his hand
today I overheard someone say "No,
I think you have just the right amount of guilt"
I don't know if it's always the same homeless bohemian
which is a comment on the vague curiosity and cruelty of life,
I leave my whole lunch near his hand, and now
we have to buy a new thermos.
I guess I'm not a person with so many deep interests, well, maybe
too bad for me. But there are a lot of things through a day
that make me wonder, walking around.
I think, I wonder why they painted that whole thing white?
I think, I wouldn't imagine they made boots like that for a person so skinny,
I mean, to fit so tight around her bony calves.
How much does it cost to have boots made
I wonder why bother?
I think, It's easy to get the idea that things matter more than they do
I am beginning to see the day without thinking *Would that were mine*
I am becoming a little more patient
which is good, considering
the quality of public transportation these days, I think
what's that person over there doing?
Oh no!

Watermark

There was a form of opening outward in our thinking,
which seemed very real and became
a thing that one person
could actually give to another, this lasted
for a long time, until it lost some of its liveliness
and grew a little crazy, without change, into a sort of abuse, nearly
gestural, though there can be no blame in it, the night
gathers into its hours the stars and your coming home
in and out of the light of each post, your speed
is a naming that draws
those white lines across the sky, pulling day
through its sieve down around you until morning, now
the anxiety shakes itself off
again, to be remembered only obscurely
as a stat, a phrase,
in the odd wake-up calm, lemon-tasty, and coffee,
an old friend
reappears, and you allow yourself the thought that
this is the one who can really know me, somehow
the patience you must find
is right there, like the light in a pumpkin, it is given
over to you to understand the pictures
through their touch, the singing lessons ask more
        questions than they answer
to you, shy horse,
day after day my door has been open, and I'd say now
nothing has changed, I have been nocturnal and that
altered nothing also, it only
made the superstitions worse, he
removed his boots to collect mementos
that could be brought back, into glass, and another
plain meaning, hyphen or adjunct

Any letter standing still and floating

So that then there is not one
and that is an easier comportment

the which does not come to harbour at dusk
but wears its own night, mayflies, barflies

hum and dum, red shore
after drifts no moon, sleepy lids, the moon

is an entirely different kind of moon, is it, languid
supine, serendipitous, a temperature

does not harbour, is not cold, chants
light in its own ear

I tell myself that at many points along the way I could have come
to understand better, come to a better understanding, if I had just
thought to, or been able to, make myself stop and look. But then to
look how? As though I was someone else? Could that have been
possible? To stop the movement and say "oh yes this," or "oh, so it's
like that." It has been a long time since I've felt such assurance as to
be able to stand back, far off, and not be taken along by the flow of
whatever given that may cross my path.

It seems that somewhere along the way I gave up the capacity for that looking. It came to feel as though I was being spoken to directly, in a kind of infusion, by everything. By the reflection of neon in the wet streets at night, or the rain itself, or by someone's sudden, odd gesture. And of course I can't tell you now what was said to me. I forget even the feeling of it, which I suppose is really all the language that was ever used. But I remember that there was a wonderful, warm, mysterious quality to it all, probably from not knowing exactly, and not asking those questions. Not feeling any need for the answers. And I can tell you that often while walking along the streets I have felt more than one person come over me, in a way, come into me, as though my skin were their skin, my face became their face, and I would suddenly find myself walking in their manner. This is what I had taken on.

It's curious now, that when I try to recall my life, what always comes back to me immediately are instances of walking, as though my whole life had taken place in that action. Of course this isn't true. I was never such a walker.

But I can remember so clearly walking down toward Old Montréal, early in the morning before we left the city, through the chunks of two walls left over from a demolished building, which had become a parking lot, and then moving out into the open of the Place Royale, looking down toward the harbour. And I remember walking home very late one night, almost dawn really, over the mountain and down Park Avenue, with my suit in a plastic bag over my shoulder.

It occurs to me now that I may remember these times so vividly because they are the moments when I woke up, so to speak. They may contain exact moments, I would have to go into it further than I'd like to be certain of that. The rest of it was a kind of dream.

I would be walking, it seems always so quiet, passing no one, and slowly the reflection of light, or the smell of the grass, or the dampness on my shoes, would take hold, and pull me along, into something like sync with myself.

The simplest moments became a sort of dance for me.

I guess this is what I'm thinking of when I say I like to be alone.

You see, I am concerned about my memory. I feel as though it's going. I'm losing something of it. Not the events which happened, I could root around and make a list of those, and I don't think I ever much knew why things happened the way they did anyway, but I am losing the how of how it felt. And as this is removed from the past, I suspect that it leaves the present as well. Memory has grown into something like a camera. Stopped, and so, manageable moments. Pictures I can see clearly still, and find some meaning and emotion and faith in them. But as soon as it starts to move, everything falls into chaos. And I turn away, unable, maybe, too tired to watch. All a blur.

And I know that in some funny way I have reversed myself, yet only to come out at the same end. To see again how blue the sky is, say, when it is very blue, sky-blue, and let it enter me. Come over me. How blue I know so-and-so's eyes can be.

I am troubled by the fact that I find I can't describe certain people. I have taken lately to sitting home at night, I'm allowed one tall glass of scotch, and slowly describing to myself all the people I know. When I come to those I care for most, I go blank. There's no beginning.

Shall I describe their hair? Their eyes? The tones of voice would be closer somehow, though still not enough. I want a word, even a sentence, that would make clear and teach me what I want to learn from them. And I'm coming to suspect that maybe this doesn't exist, or is much simpler than I'm ready to admit. I'm afraid I've fallen into a kind of mysticism, and what I'm thinking about is really as much a shadow at the back of my own mind.

I get tired. My attention falters, which may mean that I'm closing in on something, and perhaps would rather wander off. But actually I'm safe enough here, a kind of retiring witness picking up my shirts from the cleaners and spending an hour or two in the afternoon sitting in a bar with a long glass wall to watch the sidewalk.

There are so many deflections.

At the to, to a, if to, or to, and. To. As. To and, or. A as to to, and the of.

For. To as to, in a of. The of in the at, or the, or by. And of to. The of, the. A to, and. For the. And the, in a, as, and in. On.

To, to of, as in. Of. A.

So, in the the, the of a, a, and the of, the. And, the and, in a.

To so the, so to. To to of. The of a of.

Walk, seem, pass, hold, pull.

Become.

Guess think say like be.

See, am. Feel is. Lose, make, think know happen do, is feel. Is remove, suspect leave. Grow. Stop. See, find. Start, fall, turn, tire.

Know have, come. See is, is, allow. Come.

I can hear your voice as you slap your knee, *Il-mhadofie!*

I can hear your voice sort of smoking words like debris, lustrous powder, a kind of magic.

I can hear your voice splashing all over with words like wonderful.

Really.

Oh really?

Really.

Marvelous blue paper.

And phrases like 'I have the idea that' make me want to laugh, thinking of where they come to me from.

Well. So.

Spoon dance

"The bird a nest, the spider a web, man friendship."
— WILLIAM BLAKE

The sea was a pale emerald and cold both day and night but
      there was a warm, comforting smell throughout the
         corridors of the mansion, it's good
to know that someone's always cooking,
the days were long, walking in the fields, picnics,
in the evening there was reading, they joked
of a convalescence, a home, clearing an end of the great
      mahogany table,
blankets, letters that were never sent,
a bottle of Spanish wine, a hickory fire,
the white tokens of the simplest forgetfulness
beginning again its gradual advance
on a carpet of creased paper

Slowly, with that sense of having heard a sound for a long time
before beginning to listen again

One winter everyone in the neighbourhood was left alone
in every room, the light was lowered
the drapes drawn, and now
for our auguries to come true,
street after street, the construction workers
appeared as the deepest tenderness

A long face of thinking walked quietly back to the gate

The empty framework of doors and winds, the winds
whisper there, they hung
bits of glass from string in their garden
they cut themselves off from so many things, a long face
of patience was called back to the gate,
they put a mattress in the garden, though no
banners are given in the pale sky, there is enough
for you to carry home at dusk

The spindly clouds are as slow as sleep

In one view the bodies surface and there is a message
at the front desk, just as
they turn all is spent and you turn also
into the foliage by the window

The wall, the chair, the floor
the kettle, the glass with leaves
the thought about the life they were living

There are trees here, flowers, the sea,
a surprising solitude in the stream of your family
at dusk, in these hours
and later, creeping
around the hotel in the moonlight like Proust,

a slow, deferential use of the language
has come into their speech,
it's surprising too how well you've come to fit
your reputation in the family album

Newspapers in a heap on the floor by the bed
books, apples, glasses of melting ice

Does one feel any closer in knowing
a little private knowledge
a number of private appearances,
in the letters there is eventually
no solution, they are so much walking
through all I'd have liked to say to you, thinking I guess
to be understood then as though that
could nail down all the coming years

The walls stand tall and dumb as clothing

A book with a blue cover
a book with a photograph of a garden
three lawn chairs at a low, white table
a pitcher of clear liquid, two crystal glasses
slices of orange

I am burdened with meanings, I am weary with omens,
I've a woman who comes to me with her sweater on backwards
I want to simplify
everything, things to be
just what they are

I am learning to live like a foreigner
in my own city, the city where I have lived
all my life, oh I envy the travelers, imagine
what their lives must be like, still
I don't seem to be leaving, and while money
is certainly a consideration, a cause
for some alarm really, there's also something else,
probably neurotic, that keeps me here

Lately I have begun collecting maps, green
and blue as water

It's not that I want to be a tourist
I envy them only when they're two, and lovers
passing through as though it were a sort of wonderland,
but that's another story, I'm thinking more of the
ones who move to another country, stay for months,
a year or two, they rent an apartment, learn the language,
make friends, find some sort of work. The ones who are
able to throw their own history out of context

I want to live as though I were in Iceland, or Germany, or
Italy. I want to walk home at night along the roads I've
walked so often, shrugging off their knowledge. I buy
newspapers from other cities to read in cafés as though I
were in Glasgow, or Paris, but Paris is easy, Warsaw,
Ankara. There are times when I succeed, suddenly everything
is new, the process opens up, fills with imagination.
A world I've never seen before

Colours posted on every door
the conjuring trick, almost as calling up
a tone of light you've seen once and have
forever after, it creeps into your sleep,
into a kind of far-headedness that won't easily
be leaving you now,
thinking will be a big part of this, waiting also,
but before you knew what was happening, already
they'd a name for it and that door
might as well have been shut tight to you

A long face of watching walked quietly back to the gate

Sanding wood, polishing it
like a Greek's stone, I was watching her
stirring her coffee, it went on and on, I thought
she'd never stop, it seemed aimless at first, but
it was like casting a spell, holding off spirits

And our lives come down to us like rain

These acts of turning back
still occur (where the mirrors,
in their own peculiar, lively sort of light
suggesting another colourful, bright
stream of belonging, outside all the foolish questions
that are seldom actually voiced, though I think
heard all the same, stand
looking in at one another)

There's no easy way to come out of it
in the clear, one seems almost
lost to those nervous evasions that occur long before
you can choose anything better, it's curious, an interesting
phenomenon, leaving all the night trees
for later, in solitude, trying to find now
what I think I would still like to give you, and what I suspect maybe
I'd better keep for myself, even the air now
sings it, what's your name summer child, where's the locksmith
and where's the candlemaker, what might
have grown in your seeing up out of the water did in fact
root itself by the window, falling now
maybe just a step behind, closing
into this life we've wrapped of our forgetting

In cities without evening

Isn't it rather difficult for a man
to keep quiet? I have the tape of your voice
and I play it often. I am thankful for the hindrance
you've put my way. Hear the night? Finally
I worry, in autumn
I took it down to match the wall
no longer so warmly graced
I would like to learn another way to approach you
who are so often with me, in my thoughts
along the roads here that we walk, I feel funny imagining
my furrowed brow and how
that must seem to you, have you forgotten how long
my arms really are? I still like
those bright colours as I seem to recall them (the red
hat and coat, for one) in the rice-paper morning, oh no
I hadn't meant to speak like that, the crisp
tinge or tingle in the air

She was good to Pooh

He was lumbering and there were two
big brown bears wearing collars and ties and pork
pie hats and their awkward dancing
became quite graceful and he knew
that this was her doing for only she
could cause such a thing, it was a trick she played
by changing the light, he could balance
on his unicycle and his voice
improved with the singing, he placed a Mason jar
down on a hill and she filled it.
He has asked me recently if I knew all this
and I replied that by the asking he'd
confirmed my suspicions, and he asked me
if I knew what's come of her since, and I said yes sir
she's my baby now.

Dwayne's poems

1 We are afraid

We are afraid of the air that we breathe
We are afraid of the water that we drink
we are afraid of the fish in the water that we drink
we are afraid of mercury, we are afraid of our own additives,
we are afraid of produce,
we are afraid of red meat, we are afraid of white meat,
we are afraid of cows and chickens
which is absurd, considering how much they should be afraid of us, as a group
we take ourselves for granted, we slide over our fear
but we are afraid of any individual who doesn't remind us of someone we
    already know
we are afraid that cell phones give us brain cancer
we are afraid that cell phones give us ovarian cancer, this is a list
that could go on forever, I know, call me,
we are afraid of our fear,
but once you go down that road, we are afraid of our mood disorders,
but sometimes that's the only thing that makes us real
we are afraid of ourselves, I am afraid
to be part of this group that tells me I am my own worst enemy
when really I always thought that was you.

2 Spam poem

Dear Dwayne, your name is no accident
You are my twin!
silly you, click now, look out for number one
be a bedroom business master
Is she would value your male cost, how much would that be for you?
Upsize your manhood
Conjugate like a hero!
We are selling medicines for very exact as original
SATISFY ME INCREASE PENIS 1–3+ INCHES
have a easier time making her be in vanguard of loving mastery
augment your male tool
the new day is here
be a passionate sinner. Hello outlay less together with me
build the breast you have always dream of today. Make your life stressless
add power to your man's hammer delivery delayed
She delayed. To a small tobacco-pipe mast
this is a fast improvement to all qualities that make your partner say wow
Get hard-on of one passing thought
make manhood colossal
one procedure to shock your darling
such a strong positive effect on your dude-pole and only $2.00 to pay
This night your bedroom will be jungles and you?
Wild tiger!

3 Plain Dwayne

It's funny how we can recognize some people just by the way that they move,
aren't we all descendants of fish who flopped up on the ground and walked?
What makes you so different?
As plainly as I can say this,
I like to see you coming toward me,
and I usually watch you when you leave.
Here, I could say a little about the shape of your knees when you're walking away.
I like it a lot when you meet me at the bus stop on the corner.
That's a good day for me.

4 You are the black of night

You are the black of night, lingering
over the houses in the inflections of fire which is just morning approaching,
each house is a simile for us, each room, space is only an image.
You are the black and starry night, enveloping the buildings with one simple
  remark
You'd better decide who you are. And now?
Now who are you? Now? Well
This is how it seems to me:
You are the absolute black of night, fallen softly over the objects in this room
you are the blackest contextual black of the softly starlit night, you are
the blackest contextual black of the softly starlit night
and I am walking through you and the dawn is innuendo at my back, my shadow
moves on the ground before me, I am the Neptune Hotel standing
in the absolute black of the softly starlit night.

5 For example

Your fingers are long and thin and the colour of my heartbeat
Your fingers trace lines across the sand,
Your fingers draw astonishing moments
Your fingers curl slightly, your nails
tapping the surface of existence
clear and hard
And you are not patient
Your fingers are my phenomenological refutation
Your fingers are more than my memory has brought to the surface
Your fingers are the directions
Your fingers are this night
Your fingers are the sounds of the wind through the trees in Rome
Your fingers stretch across a month of afternoons
And the doors swing open and are tied with string
Your fingers are the breeze soothing the spine of a stupid talking head
Your fingers are the technical healing of electrical patter, silence
Your fingers are the arrows of voyages
That are never said out loud
I am curious and I wonder about disappearing and
Your fingers with one oval silver ring trace a long suggestive line across the map
from here to, say, anywhere along the Atlantic coast
your fingers covered with the taste of sea salt

6 A little poem about the rent

I've got to watch every dollar,
I should watch every hour too.
Money flows like time through a hole
in the pocket of my jeans, like a hole
in the pocket of my head. Whole days and weeks go by
in nickels and dimes and it's already August.
Rent is due.

7 Raise your hands

We are the ones who don't hold our heads so high in the air,
if you know what I mean. Know what I mean?
We are the ones strangers try to sell bicycles to at 3 o'clock in the morning.
Who has money at 3 o'clock in the morning?
We are the ones who have no money at 3 o'clock in the morning,
and this is really not much less than we had at 3 o'clock in the afternoon.
We are the ones who count the holes in the tiles in the ceiling
because meaning doesn't take all fucking day,
something else does. It's something else that grows stronger
by sucking the life out of everything around it.
We are the ones who have twitchy relationships.
We are the ones who are not still waters.
We are the ones who wonder how that guy's story ends.
We are the ones who know what unwanted attention is all about.
We are the ones who are failures in the system of everyone's best efforts.
We are the ones the computers worry over,
are we still out there or have we finally disappeared?

Basic modern drifting

The initial comparison does not fit the description
the description does not fit the forthcoming decision
and so the comparison is no decision at all

You roll about like a bee in the grass, one
would like that
but there's no and no other

This is coming to stand by another name
this is silence sitting on the porch
playing with the folding hands

Carpet to floor lamp, come in, clip clop, later
the slowest verbs reach back to midnight, pencil in
how they love its memory's hands

In canary time

Hat overpowering figures
carpet and blanket to your crows and rivers
proportionate twice of slight already
blue hand, black dress
salt, white
parallel theatre, middle
simplified speaker, the elusive period
of influence cloud used
to activate held and motivated using
harp, linotype, picture, train, trunk
drum, ostensibly highway driver and smaller

★★★

Side range of useless in lateral speed

Field concurrently to repeat to be grounded to understood

The methodologist will insist to this standpoint fattening

About the same time operated the triangles

Aren't obviously epoch given one looks is it because toward

Alterations or additions our rabbit repeated ten thousand times

***

Sought effects register
atmospheric tones for the ceiling
with organization and his companions
the third manner plane
closed in minimizes the most
intense colours are now in the shadows

Simply the scale of uniform infusions
for a discussion considered two
illustrate as within the constant are
occurred throughout the draperies
morning of the fog pest
highly modified heritage components

***

Often used in place of these are
vertical proposed intensity
some of the recent mattresses
in translating from nature, indelible
can be made to look the same stands
imagining will in part be reflexed
finally reaches the eye
emphasis as the wavelengths become longer
between v and r inclusive combine
is not included by some
neutral or designate all possible gravity
can similarly separate phenomenon
makes up the total dominant attribute since
into white or brown

Every other answer

Yes of the exits yet
one asks, and the wish is granted
and I hear later that I am happy with this
though a little confused as well, sometimes
one can be mistaken in preparing
for those exclusions along the sides

So much kindness in the curiosity
and one must as often stand to wait when the water
will pour in over everything, with a cool breeze
through the screen, slipping
into the dark and the stars, I am still
not quite yet ready for walking, then later again I am

II

Points north of A

Assume a void

Assume a void exists without
the hands of your own need, and already
something moves toward filling it,
so even in that silence you can trust
plain song, what felt like nothing, becoming.
The character of that silence moves out into the clear
of the valley, the lights, the silence
is of listening before you go on, as it comes
into your head, a young girl's sleepy eyes closing
at midnight, dreaming
the attraction of things, the mountains, the lovely
textures of the distances she will travel. Someone sings
her, and she dreams my whole world, the song
mustn't end before the dreaming.

Points north of *A*

Each morning the tone only
comes out assured, the over-riding
knowing and producing itself the way a season
does its days,   and the climate
grows nameable, and we are hoping,
and without denying the reasons things
got to be as they are,
to curl out of this tomorrow today.

Points north of A.
Our old suggestions, ideas in the birds'
flight, of further freedoms,
the romances we can identify
by those we
pour down our throats, cool or hot nectars and scents
taking shapes to
ring through the land of whatever, all
available or required distances'
slowly curving lines and crannies,
to reach you by way of the eye; like bells,
we can make known the grace of it
with the names for our people, descendants
of memory.

Little blue photographic
chance, it is always true
Cadillacs?
But motion over-deems —
the air between the verbs
develops its own verb,
                    the dutch white
of the fence in the sun, go way up
and look again from there.

No wind in the weather
no deposits today in duneland, the walker
walks
negative, melancholy
dreamer
to only see
the object world, denying so much.

The piling on eventually requires
that we lay off, standing way back in the corner
let things unfold
as they will, as the life of it will
and call you in. You?

Of people, of birds in the water,
of afternoon to evening,
vehicles first can be seen from far down the road:
the activities take place
at the foot of a hill, the town
in the valley
painting the fences
white

From the dance in the barn on Saturday night
taking it outside on Sunday. The orders of the rainbow
do not deny us,
even the shapes of the pebbles
smoothing beneath the bridge.

There is a piano

There is a piano, which is
an old photograph on a hill, soft focus, full of
suggestions. What would you have said to Trakl anyway?
Icons of his sister and muddy boots, his fondness
for loud minor chords in the lower registers.
Far off the hill a car moves, he says
its round white eyes cork the night, he mumbles something
which you interpret as 'Grete',
horses in the moonlight are all long legs and necks
bent down to the lake for water,
the moon's reflection at their heads,
as you approach they run off, he says, vanish
with the moonlight,
leaving the crickets to hold down the dark, and all around them
is soft chaos, full of suggestions

A birdcatcher tuning his guitar

Motion through April. Each block
is carefully watched.
The escorts appear on their own chosen cues.
You were waiting, but never knew
when it would come, and it can hardly matter
where it will take you, let them, another amendment
to the constitution in that kind of May–September romance
of what you've always wanted and what you now feel you
can rightly expect.

These days, to be out on the street
isn't as pleasant as it once was. A little knowledge
is desire. A hazy
idea of shapings to come, memory supplying
beginning, tacking the vague aspirational tones to a sure
old manner of evening, even badly lit. The future's ground
seems someone in a field
calling in all directions, calling all directions,
and waiting, pulling in objects out of corners of the room,
possibly just before the afternoon's steam
dissipates totally into an aimless circling,
a picking things up and
putting them down at other angles. Air
rushes in through your wide-open windows.

It's exactly that wind of things
you find so tough to get around or support
in this morning principle of approach
the clear head
hard and blue
forms become suggestible through the fog, motion
engages counter-motion, whatever it is, things fight
each step of the way, and this pressurized slowness also
does its part in bringing the margins
closer on the activity.

Yet this is the season of the truly possible, and
nothing can ever be forgotten until you've made
some sense of it, even then
it will turn up again but you'll have
place for it in the good order
of the transport line. Each excursion is an attempt
at collection, amassing the gasses necessary
to have an atmosphere, the hemming-and-hawing effort
of building a poem that could be at least fifty-fifty,
outside-in. Can that
be anything? What is the sound of the box you'd construct
of the sticks you've found? Parallels, diagonals
and perpendiculars only matter in visual circumstances
while other things equally have their situations.
When you look far down the street
it seems to turn to water, though you know...

But you can worry about it too much,
becoming inept at just the simple things of living
on the social level, walking along the street brings on
too many doubts, and for the most part there's not much room
for obsession strapped onto your friends.

Quiet carrying its stick. It seemed
there was no call for the catalogue
now headed by black woman with her hair
tied on her head in the traditional African manner. That
became a kind of poem too, they fell like the rain
in a curiously un-japanese garden.
When you move fast all you can feel is your own blood
pounding, but that isn't necessarily
the time when you are most alive. And while
the naming process becomes suspect the question still remains
today as yesterday, what name
would bring you closest this time?

Downtown a company has constructed a ladder
which stretches straight into heaven.
We've reserved two spots on it for tomorrow. The reason
the street seems to turn to water is the conjunction
of the angle of light with the angle
of your own vision.

The lines had been dropped, and now again
are spread across the table, you know
how time passes
and during that time you
did not exist in the clean array of this room. I'm saying
I wasn't here but I've come back, you go
out to make a call, and poof! you
aren't home for a week. Yet it can
slip back easily within the slow
ever-going-on or simply the continuable,
ideas of shapes and colours
pulling themselves into the composite of days
on the back of intention. You can only listen, really,
when you threw out the names you threw away
the string, wanting to find
that then the parcel
slowly falls open, or unfolds like a bloom to the light
in the enveloping middle of the thing.

Where the swimmers are singing from all parts of the globe
you can chart them, you need them,
you can feel they are present,
they come through the mail to you,
they come up in conversation,
they are waiting for your surprise like billboards —
you go looking for them.

An endless column of remembrance. Swans
pulling it vertical in their procession
with the trees hanging
not high over their heads in the cool shade.
The old arguments still thicken the air, even
without mention. You have mastered the coding
of your practice and can set them off
with only a look. How
we need the new light on it. The wall
becomes easier and easier to scale, but once up there you see
how impossibly wide it really is.

Circling. 'The wind encircling us
speaks always with our speech.' You are
making it up as you go along.
The nooks and crannies grow human. There's nothing out there
that you're not hearing, or there is:
you had wanted it to suggest itself
up out of nothing and to teach you
a new mode of address, yet always in the end
this old kind of non-form, or the simplest of forms,
has to do. With slow, small
alterations to the beading of the thread
in each day's noise. The idea of examination
is itself already understanding, questions
seem to answer themselves. Inside the package
is another package, and another:
they turn to sticks, and with such loose beauty
we make a box.

III

For the coming surface

"That the past is without opinion"

That the past is without opinion
would be nice, a person could
paint one another, you hear
of the rumours but
wafting through the kitchen smells

We are standing near these days
though the portrayals have always been later
mornings by the window, somehow
maybe they're right but
I don't think so, on a good day
he could put so much into that distance

A pose of nature

It'll grow clear and pale
as the sky, it seems
that all the far-away is here with us now, laughing
at how little we can actually make use of,
were you disappointed? That's
not there, what you've wanted so much
to see changed

The air was very quiet in Madagascar,
they said it was the moon, the dust
lay flat and no one said a word,
and I thought it seemed like that here too, the way
we can give one lulling activity precedence over
all the more troubling others, and make ourselves think
things are then how they appear, you said sometimes
I feel so much distance surrounding us, and on those days
there's nowhere left to run, but maybe
the trouble has been in running too far, when I still need
a place to go to now

That old story, lamps and figures
in the road, and now I guess it's me,
all the confusion in each little move, tangled
with those things that after a while it seems maybe better
not to know anymore

That will become clear and fade, I suppose
you'll stand in some other spot
and the simplicity of things will strike again, now

as a wonderfully funny joke
on your own fickleness, how it was, so
lucid and right, one then is free
to return to it, needing less and I guess in that way feeling
like you're being given so much more

I am waking early or late and I am walking quite a lot
I am always wanting to be
where you are, in the naïve trees
blue with cold, a few things get done and there are still
many more to do, the sky
has an array of colours, I am sending them all
back home to you

In the evening on the Spanish streets
the old bell's ringing, he has
more than he said he'd ask for and yet
now he wants to have more, brought over once again,
when all the fringes drop away
and the cloth of our breathing to warm us

What are they thinking, as one thinking, as if
long stretches of time could be distilled into something
a little more manageable without becoming less,
they're remembering the streets at dusk
and the sun on her shoulder as she moved, he's dreaming
and now I'm dreaming too, with his hands
in the air, believing in that music

Of a forest of intentions
greeting him, where a thing like animal fluidity
strolls through, pulling in, and giving out
the point of reference, again and again, until
you get it right, until
you stop forgetting every time you have to turn away
and night comes down a little bit lower than you'd like

Hello from Snow Park

To construe a term as true of,
addition, available
cues, light
still shines down brightly on the distance
from confusion, let the world have
those movements that it needs

There was a long walk out
at morning, and by evening you
could almost say you
'found yourself' back
home again, in the black and white world become
correct physical properties
tension and texture throughout, these situations
where he wonders how he'd happened
to have volunteered
then he tries the experiment of echoing

For a long time I used to get up early
and it was my greatest pleasure to watch the sun's
first rays shine into the room
while I drank my coffee and
calmed the dog from his obsessive howling at the cracks
of the house's old bones in the wind

It's a fine mystery
putting the night to good use,
and would gold complete it?
Straight yellow of day
in the blue sky,

there's a clumsy little pirouette
the clown does as he first enters the ring,
this seems a pleasant and simple way for him
to go into his act, a silly
bit of a wave to the crowd, gently
drawing them into the circle with him

We have grown into a style of doubting
and now there's a bleakness closing off
the end of the block,
one would repeat another
allowing personal variation to inform it
as a leg moves
through an arc and what the eye then
remembers seeing

Without colour, without body
or name nor angle of light, the month
is too reasonable a room and description
the peripheral line, a distant
and rumpled thought
as vague as the colours of your floor I do paint
from there to my door

"I grow a little weary of the talk"

I grow a little weary of the talk, the vegetable
animal and mineral of the thing,
from that was rust
through to an easier kind of friendliness,
moonlight is one
still catalogued, but sunlight now
runs on late into evening, clear and hard, it seems enough
to hear the rustle a new wind draws
through the trees, and feel somehow what that
has to do with you, silence
shimmers over our forebodings like water, and yet
there's so much there worth going after

A poem for the coming surface

Privately, even at this date, white is nudged with blue
as arrival is brought out from the duskier tones
memory has, shaded all transparence,
in the past you'd felt that these were the best times
to be near the sea, and walked away
but now there are indications that time is carrying on
those old facts, of which you'd only forgotten
how they were

White is nudged with blue, the arrival
is brought out from the duskier tones of memory
where even transparence is shaded,
in the past you'd felt that these were the best times
to dream, and gone off, but it may not be such a dream,
lately there are indications that the old facts
still carry weight

Held you and now are you
or now define your truest moments,
long past any visionary experience into a more
down to earth truth, stepping off
even the frailest of wishes into a flat hard horizon,
angles suggest miracles, so the smoother the better, all
the slow curves of long term involvements

Something could be verbed out in a number of ways, over
a length of hair we made dinner
and we walked hand in hand through the park,

another tells of something
watching from behind a thing
just out of sight, or something follows
a wide arc around the house in the country
it's too quiet to notice but you believe it's there

He fills his pail with rock from the quarry
he remembers three or four year old photographs
he tells stories with illustrations from his room
does he believe?
If we go one degree higher...
There are things in his pockets
which he gives up to see what's left
they are all colourful, what would be left?
Everything moves under angles of light

The trade gives way to laughter, salad days
support themselves, and it comes in backwards
or in another's gesture, the approach
has always been clothed in drama, which is what
you'd thought to avoid, but there are the rooms and motion is
the only way to arrive, once again the road is seen
stretching straight over so flat a terrain
as first appeared aimless

The additions have been to the periphery,
a summer room, a winter room,
a warehouse and a grass harp for entertainment,
but this is how it is, and no moment
can be completely fair,

if we go one degree higher
would there be a new dance on the hill?
A new again? Another
result of things like sand and wood
movements under angles of the sun

Does he still need the old stories?
The stone was on a morning of oldest beckonings
yet was new, there was no doubt
and never would there be regret, only
old longings where the grass had stood for him too
but water has its own old wisdom
which seems inescapable, which seems inescapable

Here too the promise is met, though
only the shortest enjoiners
turn out for the occasion, and even they
have only their moment, straight up and down like a broom handle
before it's as if they never were, funny
the words that come to mind to describe it, the face
screwing itself around with indecision, still
after so many years, in one of those moods
at the screen door, sometimes that's how young you are

One records the season, and surrounds the rock with charms,
when all else fails the approach, nightingale,
there's still nature imagery,
you can see them coming with their dictionaries
open at the page on grass
the page on birds is torn out and folded in their pockets

Silence is still too attractive to leave alone,
those who believe in magic
would come by water, are they
any more valued for that?
The rock is the rock and it's
got its own things to dream by

We pulled the blanket around us
and came home, you're to know
the size hasn't changed but we're not cold anymore,
inside the history of withdrawals is a history of approach
and the new guides are less dominant,
this seems a natural ending, pulling all consequence
into a certain order, another comfort with which to
range the skies, full of the mixture of wind
and your own breathing, and what would you feel good about
adding on?

It was cold and snowing but he waited
he counted the stars but there were so many of you
what mattered was something like sound, he said
just a minute, the grass was tall and yellowing, he walked
all the way and he's still walking
and that tells him everything
the music was on the sofa
all the clothing was with it

If we go through one more degree
scents again elicit us, and for us
a gift like perfect weather, starry nights,

to enfold us, at least the promise
is there, come upon slowly,
hours in the boat
offshore, where even our sight
protects us, though we still love our friends,
everything moves under angles of light,
does he believe? If we move through one more degree

"We have our intentions, finally"

We have our intentions, finally
which seem decipherable only at outside moments,
one can be saying one thing while
those listening watch you
act out another, and for a second there
you catch something of yourself
in the look in their eyes

You come upon it in that mirror
and those of what's left, a woman's
pins and elastics by the wash basin, or what I did
with the money that I had, or another,
a set of words aimed at some vague thing
which turns out afterward, whenever
they seem right, always the one
same thing

"In the home pieces"

In the home pieces your name is mentioned
along with the lamp on the table
of what you've given me, and I'm grateful for

Of the various tones of light in the way
the room changes through time, someone
studied you there, now one can see
what was in mind

Tuesday and another Wednesday, this land
is all an echo now, how it slopes down somewhat
where you are, knowing
what you know can only turn
that one way, the slowness the shape uses
to draw itself out, no rush, no other wishes

IV

Peeling oranges in the shade

Where we've been

Beginning with a fair woman
surrounded by dark
even on a bridge at midnight
the catfish in the water under her, all singing,
she leans closer to listen
and the boy, approached,
found her that way and
God he followed her

Where we've been is not to be
thrown up here in idle speech,
recalled by an idle mind returned,
quietly, with all acquired grace

And also not thrown up from the future now
in specifics, story-telling, inventing
others with large eyes, ears, beyond
those few who've been along
part way, so they know so much
which is enough,
and you know and I know

But it begins earlier
when he is strong without thinking
in the most comfortable of fires,
the boy stands
near her, sewing,
and tells her a story he'd heard only that morning
and warns her not to go out alone

He has always found his way home
among those things which come
simplest, lightly, fondly,
breakfast in bed, an attractive
length of hair, the word sunshine
raggedly scrawled on a tenement wall
has come easily, been easily
assimilated, leaving away the taste
for other types of existence

Carrying the sleepy child from the car
                         late at night,
into the house, everyone's own warm bed
gives light
                    leaving in the end
a completion which you sometimes
can't help but lean things up against
like the wall just inside your front door

Curiously, it has
been most constant in the body when
nonexistent in the heart — birds'
beaks and feathers, a flock
of grey sparrows flying suddenly
out from under a nun's hood

And strongest in the heart when
physically apart, water
water and form, Tuesday afternoon
or any other, passed like fingers,
a tray of drinks,
through your brain

Dark, between tall buildings
walking, toward distances which
could've been arrived at
but weren't

Tonight's tracing of lines,
another part,   without your
knowledge and consent

Much is stolen, undeniably,
thief's pleasure, a dancing bear
and a harmonica on street corners
which has never come naturally
and throws centrifugally,
a broken record which
rides as the lines of my own face ride,
that one plays often
on a variety of turntables

The need, if not that then desire
exists, through the street fights
in boots and the crouching under bushes
to examine each other's flowers,
to own and be owned, it seems,
to pass through washing machines and come out
all right, more of the first it seems,
completely but not bad,
running, it was not the place
that was too lonely and too wild, but
the hill wife herself

To have one thing matter
is to give everything meaning,
and so clutching at straws is no
foolish endeavor, but just
one way of living, of going on while still carrying on
have your cake and eat it too
as you forget even what exactly it was and
what may be

The song mentions hickory fires
oak and ash, — don't use no green
or ripe wood, it'll get you
by the smoke

Something touched then with an open palm
a love of dolphins could apply here
the sound of someone's hands clapping
from across the hall, and one who
grows roses in his yard
has cut a dozen and sends them
round to your dressing room door

Phrases from the mole column

Perplex, confuse, worry,
drudge, moisten, puddle in mud,
watered, having clouded appearance like
watered silk, this appearance,
slightly wet, damp, marked by discharge
of matter, make moist,
become moist,
water or other liquid
diffused in small quantity as vapour
condensed on surface, systems
of tattooing, serving to grind,
acting on or by means of large masses
in process of refining, treacle,
spot, blemish on human skin,
other mammals of same family, small eyes,
small mound thrown up by,
in burrowing, exaggerate obstacles,
as pier, breakwater, massive structure
or junction between places separated
by water,
artificial harbour

The seasonal has

The light goes off in a glance of fire,
only in one view toward distraction,
the same way the first and each
hot brightness fanned out to allow for
other additions to life, other days'
duties and desires

You dress for a stroll in the rain
whenever it's warm, whenever
the rain is warm you
put on comfortable clothes and take a walk,
say it's a time for thoughtfulness,
as one who was once a bolter and who now
chews his food like a maniac
tiny bites, fed and digested fully
before saying o,
                    she leaves
all up to providence

Distance is the unifier, as one
walked down the hall the appearance of things
carried the other on intact, this is always
the account, and the eventual warmth
that enters these situations
is no souvenir

Spreading the dust of a collection
of old mango leaves received
years ago in the mail, the only thing ever kept
so long, now in the throes
of its last colours, the decay is slowed
whatever way possible, frozen
at this stage and at that
for the future, or
put to a few last services before
becoming clear and meaningless

A fairy tale setting floats on a sea of leaves and flowers,
the change of clothes makes all the difference
even a small shift of placement can seem
enough to bring on parades
in the light of early attentions, ringing out the old
to the tune of those first impressions
of beauty in private activities on the roof,
the dancers come round illustrating
the possibilities

There is the sort of promise fog makes
for a row of houses
by holding back all straight lines
and giving them up piecemeal
as you continue down the block,

you want to find out for yourself
and begin by moving into one room and
storing all your possessions in another
taking them out as they prove necessary

Still, on the roof near the chimney
the moment's notice is ceremoniously posed
simple pretexts serve the more complex attributes
of even straightforward gestures
in the middle of tenses

An introduction

An introduction on the slim basis of
approximate mixtures, a certain
daily past and new present appearances,
all the horsemen in the world couldn't
put the egg back together again, but one assumes
enough to begin, having seen
a number of gestures appear elemental,
winter sun, while snow covers the streets

is the composite, his difficulty
is in the colouring, which is both
extravagant while hard-edged and
demanding, dreams and happenstance
are not prime value, one must
take on R.S.V.P.'s, in the distance
there is a movement, a circling

The attraction of highway signs
blows momentary questions universal,
he has travelled at least the week
arriving with doubts and
a few other thoughts jangling like keys
to come into pastorals,
you'll be fairly welcomed,
the god's foot describes arcs
around shepherds and taps
to the fiddler's maybe mournful tune

reinforcing your belief that
snow is beautiful in more views than post cards,
there's more to it than Christmas
or trees and wooden fences being
taken out of sight, reformations
have brought us this far
with whatever particular frosts on the ground, and years
are being held back here by a telephone voice,
the rings of trees one moment, then
the days one's gone through
which involve scratches, naturally, and small
testaments which pile up like layers
of water in a barrel

He rolls into town then in a yellow 2-door,
there are some actions on the shore
which could never be less, long ago
a perfect fit, as the ocean begins the
high-tide cycle,
sunglasses, aloe oil,
and sand between the toes, we are
going for everything and
we're shy to admit it

Deciding on a party as late as Saturday morning,
you phone at least forty people in raincoats
or Bolivian sweaters, and one from
what we could call new pastorals,
silk energy coming as a leopard, or crystal
rather than fur, full of promise

A collector

The time of day has nothing going for it
under the yellow shaded lamp
newspapers on the floor
thinking again and again of a grafting effort
becoming so important, its smooth contours,
the powder on an insect's wing,
the way out and back now grows as uncertain
as previous trades

Ice

They arrive in ships, lovely sails
in what is a sunset from where they've come
their passports are checked, you
have reached the age of reason,
they walk uphill from the harbour
and begin, call it
a march learning to walk,
along every street, it never ends
and in that reminds them of the sea

To which we can now add the image of
floating free, adrift in space,
that kind of dry ice of the heart, where
journeying is the wrong word
as it intimates destination

As though this and as though that
not quite enough one to negate any other,
as though a time period were ending into a future
uncertain beyond that it will be another time period
in which to wrestle with the season's insistencies
and personal assumptions, the trees sway
in any moment's wind, you'd be grateful
for even slight continuations, stumbled over
like a sudden scent of wet grass
bringing to mind again other times
entirely other movements of faith
and ways of thinking

This is the mood of the hour,
an old sweetheart, suited to winter, to patiently
approach the areas of possibility believed inside
the whole ball of wax

The lost first words rode a necessary brashness
whistling upwind, each at once this and as
tentative as every singular letter   a   b
punched into place across the white surface
as another day requires another
show of hands in the crowd
at a moment neither favourable nor unfavourable

The ice factions off blue light
reflects white, hanging outside the window
cold hard fact producing itself
on the edge of our central heating

The stone does not incorporate
a theory of sculpture as the chipping away of
excess, uncovering the sculpture,
conversations grow longer
with having to backtrack and beat
all around the bushes, ready to leap
on whatever shows its head in the dust

The fence

(1)

The urge is now nine parts desire,
peeling oranges in the shade
of the future's I.O.U.'s, waiting
for your contact to turn up with the new map,
in other words when every day is Sunday
the road from the park comes by here, or
all through winter trains arrive at noon
on sunny days, four o'clock
during storms, and each car is numbered

The path through the hills is feathered with artificial carnations
which run down the troughs in the rain
soggy paper and a mixture of dyes turned finally
one colour, flooding the in-roads and sinus like so much
alternate construction, you learn to appreciate
the patience of smoke

(2)

Something said in another context
reminded you how long you'd been here,
thinking you were pacing expressively and
in a way you were, however
those with the whiskey on their breath
say they're most there when least there, and now finally
you can choose the same for yourself,
though only the decision is simple, seeming to incur
a slowing down when already
the leaves are fidgeting in distrust

(3)

The invitations go out halfway through
the second or third rainy day, in direct
proportion to it and your own low profile,
any other week stacked under
a wheel's turning now, coming full circle
either too fast for you to jump off
or you didn't jump off or you turned it
into an accord, as though blinding could change
even the light

(4)

Luck has become matter of fact, again
the exit proved timely, allowing another glimpse
of what you'd always taken as free-ing
at face value, the examination
in corners of the room is a more recent development
equally liberating, though one gives towards the other and
the encompassed area is what's yours
coming to sense in addition

At this point most acts
seem to land like birds in protocol
as the face of it is lost and found in impressions
and the rich dark off-reds
enfold again what is momentary, taken
as one more assurance

A number of past considerations
made sense in other ways and were quickly included
into gestures become civil as trees, tying
any rain in with any mountain, casting those
mirror-like images and twice told tales
through themselves, to reshape
with new quirks suggesting new resemblances
which are already forming a verb among the colours of trees and houses

Line of incidence

There's something to the predictable, this is
never more apparent than by the sea
which is beautiful, all your dealings
come home at night in relation to that,
and if gestures compensate then one will always
know moments of such turning
toward the horizon with wide eyes
and a lowering of approximations

We became increasingly human
at the festival, sea, sand, and the sun,
but the horses are not to be ridden
they are loose out where the road winds down
from the hills through the trees
to the ocean which is not for drinking,
perhaps this achieves another final simplification
as free as birds are when there's no birds around

"Saliences"

At the far point of the line
we're approaching the other end of
is a chance-principled arrangement of rocks
which the sunlight hits at angles
through a shade of birds flying over
the momentary effect is imagined, reasoned
a rumbling in the tubes
someone speaks up, that's the first component
and the angels go back from religion

An optimistic watch

The night is deadpan, is static
in the iridescence of a single element
now beginning to hold forth where
all old grown too accustomed virtues had been
and had held, through what could've been
less disturbing without certain assumptions

The division goes on whatever
let the motion of the waves relax you
those fires in the far away distance
indicate subjects for another day's frolic
and you must be rested and wise
when you chance to meet them

Ode to an urn

If one is around the corner
and one is out front, how much is known?
the door closes itself
out of time we are whiskers
defined by feet, this may be true
such approximations are rain
when the green drought grows all around

So decrees initiate themselves
into the contrary value of stars, vouching any other
idea for continuation, substitution,
come through here once your story's unwound
come through the gauze of the curtain

Gulls again fly out of sight by flying over the wall
these are the long lasting possessions
while one season draws away from the next
all motions too often elucidated
toward the river, the same old show
has its precedents, it's enough to say we
know what to expect, have come so far
with our accord, even that we'll reapply after a few tunes

Sentiments of orange

Starting up again, the whispers
like sand blown against a screen
with the intimations of even the word *flower*
or the word *sand*, today also is affected by resemblances
bringing the trees into the wanting them

Orange is the colour drawn around
lightly, almost not there, but promising growth
out of the first shades of attention
inclusions are already settling, the requirements
are posted alongside the notices of change,
there is a box by the ocean for those who
want things simple and all they get is rain

People of different sizes walk by each other.
people of different sizes walk by each other
in the painting of Paul Delvaux
where thin women whose breasts are white and bare
look nowhere on the arms of men incorporated into suits
but that isn't the same, all ice
blues and whites
and this is more orange than that, so more real

Between yellow and red, orange at times seems
as close as you can get to the sun,
your eyes and hands hedge your bets
but the birds seem assured or accepting
and still are able to glide off a wind into updrafts

The old sky is given another colour
but the first wish must come true before
going on to the second
so the portrait will never be complete
draw the fine lines out from the centre
and they become circular, drawing toward another centre
which then is all that matters
your concerns have amassed themselves and that
· is your vocabulary, to which even orange is brought into the predictions

Late at night other lives have also
made themselves known, and as they repeat
have become shadows of your hesitations
most nights we would meet under the lamp on the corner
with all light drawn to your face in those true
sentiments of orange I can only approximate
or approach at the most useless hours, but then you know
falling trees make noise, so you have that at least

So you see how little you stray
and this being inside can make you happy
perhaps only until the next call is heard, but then
shadows become old friends, second nature
and return to free you back into your confines

Apostrophes transport you
along the last block into suburbia, relay the hour
to grammar, at night the sand
is much cooler to the touch, you stand
very quietly until you notice

Corners locate the tone
fading slightly, still orange is there, suppose
someone places a jar of water near the ocean,
sleeps happily all night, and the next day
brings the jar home, what has changed

V

Put yourself in my shoes

Put yourself in my shoes

A period of waiting, reading, the palms
describing the words in her eyes
as a playfulness diminishes
into smaller circles, a look
over her shoulder, a glance, the rim
of a glass lamp, and here it is already
December, the clumsy month,
I imagine you can see much of that
in my actions, to be pulled
out of absence into an old legend,
familiar, belonging

The long leaves of your presence,
the wind, the sun,
a tightness around the skin, a swimmer's
yellow dream around your shoulders,
a pattern of our movement
became apparent, a formal row of elms,
a long and winding pond
the suburban colours across a long green park
to be crossed, the hardest day,
a long summer distance,
almost speechless, one low and pearly note
for the middle of the night, these are the colours
as they were taught to me, in layers
one coming through another, mixed,
rich, painterly,

I have no clear sense of beginning
to their appearance,
it was only a matter of saying *Yes*
I've noticed for a while now, the beautiful
and pale olives, a white almost
the colour of almonds
and finally ask to sit down, so late,
so self-conscious,
a window to admit the light
and a slowness
a reticence, to learn
out of an act of listening, seeing
seeing, and repeating, suddenly
a vase of hard flowers, unexpected
in July, water
mentioned in the length of an arc, a pause
in the movement of your hand across your brow
in your quiet voice,
you were everywhere
it was this great, giddy feeling
that began to release me,
I wanted to do it right for once, happily,
I looked everywhere
where is she
tonight? Now? *You're like a cop*,
out of the dusk of evening, and
where is she tonight?

The hours grow familiar, this calm
can begin to seem enough, soon
the clearest thoughts come
when no one is listening, the texture
of this person's world
in relation to you, to emerge
patiently, completely, a jungle of a life,
a photograph of a child
but not of the man, nor of the woman,
I will draw this out from you, slowly, speaking
low, toward the ground,
the most opaque and pale waves,
shimmering bees,
the smell of grass, rain, a seriousness quietly
began to ask difficult questions,
to pronounce the words evenly,
letting them hang
in the air,
and an idea
of what could be
rose, slowly turning
up out of the earth in a field
of the most luminous flowers, the most clichéd
and brilliant images you can think of
all take part,
and in my house dreams the house
has grown so clear to me, so strong, finally my own,

this sureness can be an embarrassment
I'm becoming a Kennedy, I dream
of things as they could be
and ask *Why not*
with wild, extravagant, exact
demands, as possible as they are unlikely,
the gray lights of the streets
reflected in the snow,
a woman in a black coat walking alone
under the lights of another house,
this old Portugal of photography,
where will she go? Where will you go?

A soapstone carving of the facts, so Canadian,
smooth as skin, your shoulder, your arms, I'm trying
not to get too funky, as round
as a swimmer slipping down
into his own hypnosis, the language
of these winter rooms,
the dark and dusty shades of red,
a Persian carpet, the heavy Indian blankets,
a winter night, Christmas green,
a dangerous, numbing, cold wind
banging the windows against their frames,
a man goes out walking now, alone,

knowing what he already knows
about her, the pearly woman, and about
the worlds he carries
within himself, too, climbing
her steps with an enforced slowness,
it's almost a secret, it's almost a grin,
high as a kite, I know
I'm not stepping easy, while even the years
change, a convenient name
for this climbing
into all the possible measures
of a hard and better life

Acknowledgements

The following poems were previously published, some in slightly different versions or under different titles, in chapbooks and other publications as indicated:

"Assume a void," "Points north of A," "There is a piano," and "A birdcatcher tuning his guitar" were published as *Points North of A*, by Villeneuve Publications (Montreal, 1980.) "Put yourself in my shoes" was published as a Villeneuve chapbook of the same title in 1984.

"That the past is without opinion," "A pose of nature," "Hello from Snow Park," "I grow a little weary of the talk," "A poem for the coming surface," "We have our intentions, finally," and "In the home pieces" were published as *For the coming surface*, by Dreadnaught (Toronto, 1980.)

"Where we've been," "Phrases from the mole column," "The seasonal has," "An introduction," "A collector," "Ice," "The fence," "Line of incidence," "An optimistic watch," "Saliences," "Ode to an urn," and "Sentiments of orange" were published as *Peeling Oranges in the shade* by The Paget Press (Sutton West, 1978.)

"Assume a void," "There is a piano," "We have our intentions, finally," and "She was good to Pooh" were published in the anthology *Cross/cut: Contemporary English Quebec Poetry*, edited by Peter Van Toorn and Ken Norris, Véhicule Press (Montreal, 1982.)

"A poem for the coming surface" and "There is a piano" were published in the magazine *Atropos* (1978.) "In cities without evening," "Every other answer," "Watermark," and "In canary time" were published in the magazine *Four by Four* (#3, July 1983).

"Any letter standing still and floating," "Spoon dance," "You are the black of night," and "For example" appeared in *The New Quarterly* (2005). "All those moons" and "Raise your hands" appeared in *The Fiddlehead* (2011). "A poem in the kitchen" appeared in *Literary Review of Canada* (2011).

I would like to thank the Canada Council for a grant I received in 1980, that helped me to complete some of the poems in this volume.

Thanks to Zsolt Alapi, Peter Sibbald Brown, Michael Cameron, James Campbell, Fred Louder, Al Moritz, Robyn Sarah, and Carl Snyder. And for this book, I thank Robyn Sarah. It would not have been published without her.

About the Author

Jack Hannan lives with his family in Montreal, the city where he was born. Since the late 1970s, his poems have appeared occasionally in Canadian literary magazines or as small-circulation chapbooks. He has worked in bookselling and publishing all of his adult life.

Author photo by Deborah Shea.